MY TURN NEXT!

by

Bil Keane

FAWCETT GOLD MEDAL • NEW YORK

My Turn Next!

Published by special arrangement with The Register &
Tribune Syndicate, Inc., by Fawcett Gold Medal Books, a
unit of CBS Publications, the Consumer Publishing Division
of CBS Inc.

ISBN: 0-449-14412-7

Printed in the United States of America

First Fawcett Gold Medal printing: June 1981

10 9 8 7 6 5 4 3 2

"I think they're goin' through a phase."

"Listen to the ice tinklin' in my glass."
"That's not nice, Billy! I'm TELLIN' what you just said!"

"God does a lot of coloring in the spring,
doesn't He?"

"We want a LADIES' hammer. It's for Mother's Day."

"If you see anything up there that belongs to us, will you throw it down, Daddy?"

"Was daddy right? Did you knock out every-
body's eyes?"

"I'm out here, Mommy, raining on your plants."

"I WAS gonna say, 'I need a hug,' but I guess
I better not."

"When I grow up I'm gonna have a beard and a mustache so NOBODY will kiss me."

"Who turned on that cricket?"

"They're not whiskers. They're sunbeams."

"You've gotten big, too."

"What's for dinner, Thel?"

"I think the elevator is stuck."

"I wouldn't want to hibernate all winter. I'd miss Christmas."

"I dropped the tooth."

"New cards are nice and slidey."

"Are you refilling his eyes with tears?"

"Jeffy went to bed already and his toothbrush
isn't even wet!"

"I beat Billy gettin' dressed!"

"I just ate. Don't I have to wait an hour?"

"I'm havin' chicken on the cob."

"I was just kiddin! It tickled!"

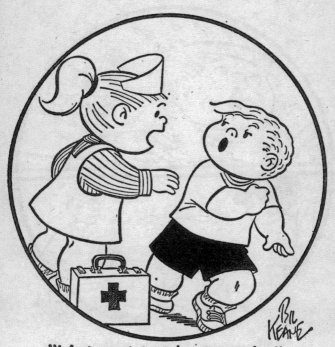

"I just want to take your pulse."
"Will you give it back?"

"Daddy, are you from the olden days?"

"I think he needs new batteries."

"One potato, two potato, three potato, four.
Five potato, six potato, seven
potato, more."

"Mommy! PJ touched the thing with his mouth!
Will he get a disease?"

"That's a hyphen. It means the word isn't done yet."

"The other three learned to say 'Mommy' first. Wonder how PJ learned to say 'Daddy.'"

"Grandma sent me $5 and I can spend it right
away 'cause it's REAL money and
not a check."

"Daddy's toe is trying to escape!"

"There's nothing in this cereal."

"Your kiss wore off, Mommy. It hurts again."

"Anyhow, Billy, it's not nice to say 'skinning
the cat' in front of Kittycat."

"Mommy, if you swat any flies will you save them for my spider?"

"Can we put some dirt and some water in the blender and make mud?"

"Wish I had a skateboard with training wheels."

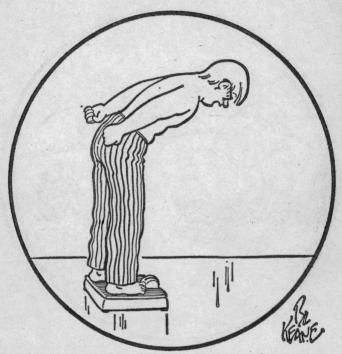

"Those kids have got to stop leaving so much
food on their plates."

"Did you hear that kiss, Grandma?"

"I'm takin' my skateboard to New York City
with us. They have PLENTY of
sidewalks there!"

"I hope the pilot tells us when we get to New
York so we don't go past our stop."

"'Tell Jeffy to stop running ahead. He just
wants to be the first one to
see New York City.'"

"Do we have to write our names or will
Daddy sign for all of us?"

"I wish they didn't have so many CARPETS
in this hotel so I could ride
my skateboard."

"Wow! We could see ALL OVER New York if it wasn't for that building next door."

"Don't keep lookin' up at the buildings!
People will know we're
from outta town!"

"Don't walk over that thing, Jeffy!
You might fall down
into the subway."

"Is it okay to drink the water in New York?
Y'know what happened to
Grandma in Mexico!"

"I wanna send this picture of our hotel to
Grandma. Will you mark
which room is ours?"

"That's the Canadian flag and the next one
is — No, that's Australian, then next
is Spain — No, wait . . . Sweden!
Then, I think that's either Italy
or Ireland and. . . ."

"Don't worry 'bout pushin' your floor,
Mister, cause my brother
pushed ALL the buttons."

"Mommy, will you hold my dollar just
in case I get mugged?"

"The TV programs here are the same as ours
at home, but the channel
numbers are wrong."

"There's the place we sightsaw yesterday."

"Daddy, tell Billy to stop callin' it the 'Umpire State Building.'"

"We shoulda brought our FISHIN' stuff, Daddy!"

"Isn't that the guy we saw on TV at the start
of the Olympics?"

"Oh, no! It's happened again, Mommy! The lady's in there startin' to clean our room."

"PJ's playin' in the sandpile."

"Aren't we gonna get goin' any faster than this?"

"Why didn't you go before we left the hotel?"

"Wow! look at all the toy cars down there!"

"Why does that man keep talkin' to us, Daddy? Does he KNOW us?"

"I hope they have hamburgers, 'cause that's
what I'm gonna order."

"I wouldn't want to be an asternaut if that's
the way it feels!"

"We HAFTA go home, Jeffy! Daddy ran out
of money."

"We have beautiful stars in our neighbor-hood."

"Sesame seeds? Do they come from Sesame Street?"

"They're wrestlin', not boxing. In boxing, you're not allowed to hug."

"The world is solid as far as I've gone."

"Read my palm, too,
Mommy!"

"After you miss a shot, you hafta look at your racket like daddy always does."

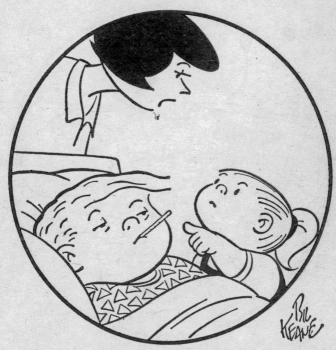

"It's not a lollipop. I'm taking his tempera-
ture."

"He's cryin' because the wolf scared him."

"The ice cream man! Can we buy something?"

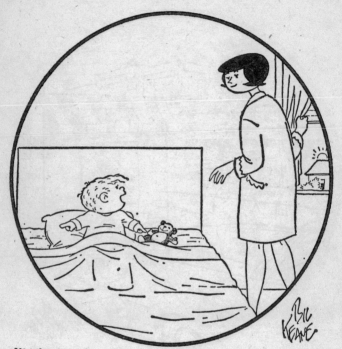

"Which side of the bed is the right side to get up on, Mommy?"

"When Daddy turns this one, the windshield
wipers start bowing to each other."

"I put some food in my tummy to cover up the empty."

"That's selfish!"

"Mommy, what shall we do with the water-mellon crusts?"

"My feet don't reach the pedals."

"Look, Mommy! My hands got OLD!"

"The sky's grumbling!"

"Now, don't touch a thing in the woods 'cause
it might be poison ivory."

"What comes after 12, Mommy? I'm 'it' for hide and seek."

"See, this is what I do to lose my sneeze."

"Now, what were we talking about?"

"They're thirty-five cents. The ice cream man says NOTHING costs a quarter anymore."

"We can't have it all the time. We have to share it with Chinese kids."

"We put a letter in this bottle, Daddy. Will you take us to the ocean so we can send it?"

"This beach has water in the cellar!"

"Do you like my new zucchini, Daddy?"

"Susan's going to visit her grandparents. They live in Concord, New Hamster."

"Will you watch my bugs for me so they don't get away?"

"This is Mashed Potato Mountain, and that's
Gravy Lake."

"That's our scale. Every morning you get on it,
then mumble under your breath."

"I found a piece of tinsel on the lawn from last
Christmas. Shall I keep it for this
year's tree?"

"Don't wash THAT shirt, Mommy! It has the autographs of all the guys in my class on it."

"Mommy, when Billy's, you know, talking to somebody, you know, he's always saying 'YOU KNOW.' Will you tell him, you know, to stop it?"

"Mommy, is Dolly made of sugar and spice
and everything nice or is she just
makin' that up?"

"He must be the instructor."

"But I only opened my eyes a LITTLE to see what you were doin'!"

"I did four chin-ups and one eye-up!"

"Grandma's needleing me a sweater."

"Mommy, is it all right to play baseball in ten-nis shoes?"

"Jeffy got a book from the shelf and it's not a
Dr. Seuss!"

"I can't wear that shirt. It's not the one
Grandma gave me to go with these shorts."

"How do you read me?"

"You can tell saints 'cause they always wear
ring hats."

"Why are we leaving, Daddy? Aren't we stayin' for the third movie?"

"Mommy! Where's that playpen we used to
keep PJ in?"

"Shall I tell Mr. Ferrell not to mow his lawn 'cause you want to sleep?"

"When you and I have children, Mommy and Daddy will be promoted to grandparents."

"We ran out of flies."

"When they get shorter, I can wear them."

"I'll bet I'd do better if I could wear TWO
skate boards."

"I don't think Dr. Cuthbertson's kids eat
apples 'cause it would keep their
Daddy away."

"When I get my wisdom teeth will that make me smart?"

"We've run out of babies at our house."

"Backpack me next, Daddy!"

"I think Jeffy has a cold. I can hear his nose snoring."

"Who ate the middle out of this cookie and then put it back?"

"Not me."
"Not me."

"Do we get presents on Labor Day?"